SQUADRONS!

No. 58

THE FORGOTTEN
PATROL SEAPLANES

PHIL H. LISTEMANN

ISBN: 979-1096490-99-8

Colour profiles: Claveworks Graphics

GLOSSARY OF TERMS

PERSONEL :
(AUS)/RAF: Australian serving in the RAF
(BEL)/RAF: Belgian serving in the RAF
(CAN)/RAF: Canadian serving in the RAF
(CZ)/RAF: Czechoslovak serving in the RAF
(NFL)/RAF: Newfoundlander serving in the RAF
(NL)/RAF: Dutch serving in the RAF
(NZ)/RAF: New Zealander serving in the RAF
(POL)/RAF: Pole serving in the RAF
(RHO)/RAF: Rhodesian serving in the RAF
(SA)/RAF: South African serving in the RAF
(US)/RAF - RCAF : American serving in the RAF or RCAF

RANKS
G/C : Group Captain
W/C : Wing Commander
S/L : Squadron Leader
F/L : Flight Lieutenant
F/O : Flying Officer
P/O : Pilot Officer
W/O : Warrant Officer
F/Sgt : Flight Sergeant
Sgt : Sergeant
Cpl : Corporal
LAC : Leading Aircraftman

OTHER
ATA: Air Transport Auxiliary
CO : Commander
DFC : Distinguished Flying Cross
DFM : Distinguished Flying Medal
DSO : Distinguished Service Order
Eva. : Evaded
ORB : Operational Record Book
OTU : Operational Training Unit
PoW : Prisoner of War
PAF: Polish Air Force
RAF : Royal Air Force
RAAF : Royal Australian Air Force
RCAF : Royal Canadian Air Force
RNZAF : Royal New Zealand Air Force
SAAF : South African Air Force
s/d: Shot down
Sqn : Squadron
† : Killed

The fortunes of war gave the opportunity for some aircraft types to play a role or fly in markings other than originally intended. With the invasion of many European countries in the first months of the war, only the British Empire remained in the fight with bases relatively safe to operate from. Many defeated airmen, often with their aircraft, found asylum at these bases. Among the aircraft which fled their original countries were patrol seaplanes. In some cases, the numbers of certain aircraft, or the fact they were simply in the right place at the right time, were enough to for the RAF to consider their use. This was certainly true for the Dutch Fokker T.VIIIs, Yugoslavian Dornier 22s and the Rogožarski SIM-XIV. Alternatively, it was often simply an order of aircraft not delivered before the destination country fell to the enemy. That was the case for the Norwegians' Northrop N-3PBs and the Netherlands' Vought OS2U Kingfishers. Those types entered RAF and RAAF service respectively but, because of the small quantities involved, they did not see widespread use; that doesn't mean they were useless though.

THE FOKKER T.VIII

Following the rise of nazism in neighbouring Germany, it was recognised in the Netherlands that military modernisation was increasingly necessary, particularly in the field of aviation. One requirement, identified in 1937 by the Royal Netherlands Navy, was for a new floatplane, for coastal defense and aerial reconnaissance, that could be alternatively armed with bombs or torpedoes. Fokker decided to respond to this specification and submitted its own design, known by the company designation T.VIII. The needs were such that the Dutch ordered five T.VIIIs in September 1938, an indirect consequence of the Munich crisis, several months before the maiden flight on 22 February 1939. Powered by two Wright R-975-E3 engines rated at 450 hp, the Fokker T.VIII had a crew of three. Its armament consisted of two 7.92mm machine guns for defence (one in a rear position and one fixed, forward-firing for the pilot) and 600 kg (1,325 lb) of bombs, or one torpedo.

As the trials were successful, the T.VIII entered immediate production. After the first five aircraft, the Dutch Government ordered another 19 in November 1939, and 12 more in February 1940, the latter being the T.VIII M, an all-metal variant; the earlier airframes were a mix of wood and metal construction. In the end, however, only 11 T.VIIIs were delivered to the Dutch before

The first Dutch Fokker T.VIII, R-1, during a test flight before its delivery to the Dutch Navy. It wears pre-war Dutch roundels, similar to the former Czechoslovakian roundels which led to the dramatic event of 13 September. Thereafter, the orange triangle was adopted as the Dutch national marking.

the country was invaded in May 1940. Later, the Germans restarted the Fokker production line and assembled a few aircraft. The Finnish also placed an order in January 1939 for two T.VIII Cs, able to operate from water and land, but it was not fulfilled. When war broke out, the T.VIII was already introduced in service and immediately began to fly coastal patrols. On 13 September, one was shot down by a German Do 18, an event which led to the Dutch roundels being changed to an orange triangle shortly thereafter. When the Germans launched their offensive in May 1940, nine Fokker T.VIIIs were airworthy and were soon spread among various bases in France. Eventually, on 22 May, eight of these aircraft escaped to the United Kingdom; notably, one T.VIII was used to aid in the escape of two members of the Dutch Cabinet.

WITH THE RAF

In the chaos that followed the fall of the Netherlands, Belgium and France, many military personnel found asylum in England. Among them were Dutch Navy personnel and some of their aircraft, of which the most useful, to British eyes, were eight Fokker T.VIIIs. Therefore, the Dutch were the first of the defeated Allied nations to form squadrons within the RAF. On 1 June 1940, Nos. 320 and 321 (Dutch) Squadrons were formed with Dutch Navy personnel, who had arrived in sufficient numbers. The former unit was destined to fly the Fokkers while 321 was earmarked for Avro Ansons, both operating from Pembroke Dock on the Irish Sea. The Fokkers and their crews had the advantage of being immediately available and operational while 321's personnel had to be trained on the Ansons.

The new squadron was placed under the command of Lt Cdr JM van Olm and logically came under Coastal Command authority. Before any operations could be carried out, some administrative tasks had to be performed for the personnel and the aircraft. Eight Fokkers were officially taken on RAF charge and received the serials **AV958 to AV965**. Anticipating a lack of spare parts, only six (AV960 to AV965) became operational with 320; the other two, AV958 and AV959, were kept in reserve to provide parts as required. The first sorties were carried out on 20 June, when AV964 and AV965 escorted a convoy in St George's Channel. The tempo was slow, however, as only 11 more sorties were carried out before the end of June, a little more than 15 operational hours. In July, these figures rose to 41 and 185 respectively, but 320 recorded its first casualty when, on 26 July, AV964, captained by OVL1 E. Martaré, was seen to dive into the sea near the convoy the crew was escorting. The four crewmen perished. In August, 45 sorties were flown, representing 210 hours on patrol, and, in September, (to the 26th) 44 sorties were flown over 200 hours. That day, the 26th, another drama unfolded when AV963, captained by OVL3 JAL Schevenhoven, failed to return with his crew from a convoy patrol. With four aircraft now available, and the lack of spare parts becoming critical, it was decided to withdraw the type from operational service with immediate effect and convert 320 to Ansons. The Fokkers had flown 143 sorties and about 610 hours for Coastal Command.

A Fokker T.VIII of the newly formed No. 320 (Dutch) Squadron RAF is attended to by Dutch naval groundcrew at is taken down to the water at Pembroke Dock.

Engine maintenance for a Fokker T.VIII. No. 320 Squadron was highly publicised during the summer of 1940 as it was important for the British to show they were not alone in continuing the struggle after the invasion and occupation of continental Europe by the Germans (even though 320's contribution at the time was relatively small).
The location of the forward-firing MG is clearly visible on the left side of the nose.

A Fokker T.VIII with RAF roundels and the orange triangle on the nose.

The remaining Fokkers were kept by 320 to maintain flying skills until the Anson program was completed; the Fokkers were then sent to Felixstowe for storage, except AV959 and AV962 which were struck off charge at the end of September as not airworthy. On 28 November, AV958 suffered an engine failure and the pilot, OVL3 WMA van Rossum, was obliged to make an emergency landing near Sudbury. Fortunately, van Rossum and his crewmate, SMJRV C. De Borst, survived the crash. The three remaining T.VIIIs, now stored, were finally struck off charge in June 1941 and scrapped

Summary of the aircraft lost on Operations - 320 (Dutch) Squadron

Date	Pilot	S/N	Origin	Serial	Code	Fate
26.07.40	OVL1 Eduard **Martaré**		RNNAS	**AV964**	-	†
	OVL3 Jan **den Hollander**		RNNAS			†
	SM Aart **de Knegt**	11780	RNNAS			†
	Kpl Johannes **Ras**	12062	RNNAS			†
26.09.40	OVL3 Johannes **Schevenhoven**		RNNAS	**AV963**	-	†
	Sgt Henirich **Akkers**	11769	RNNAS			†
	Mat Louis **Scholman**	6693	RNNAS			†

Total: 2

Date	Pilot	S/N	Origin	Serial	Code	Fate
28.11.40	OVL3 Wilhelmus VAN **ROSSUM**		RNNAS	**AV958**	-	-
	SM Cornelis DE **BORTS**	11766	RNNAS			-
	Total: 1					

Close-up of the rear gun, the only defensive weapon carried by the Fokkers.

KNOWN NUMBER OF SORTIES COMPLETED BY EACH FOKKER T-VIII

Serial	Former	First sortie	Last sortie	Nbr sorties	Op.hours	Comment
AV958	R-1	-	-	-	-	
AV959	R-3	-	-	-	-	
AV960	R-6	05.07.40	10.09.40	33	148.4	
AV961	R-7	25.06.40	20.09.40	31	130.0	
AV962	R-8	10.07.40	26.09.40	29	136.8	
AV963	R-9	15.07.40	26.09.40	26	107.4	Lost
AV964	R-10	20.06.40	26.07.40	7	17.9	Lost
AV965	R-11	20.06.40	15.08.40	17	68.1	
Total				143	607.8	

Two more views of a Fokker wearing RAF roundels. Note the small orange triangle painted on the undersurfaces near the engine nacelle. Below: note where the serial, AV961, was painted, just below the stabilisers. The previous Dutch markings under the wings can also be seen. With the RAF, no squadron codes or even individual letters were ever applied to the T.VIIIs.

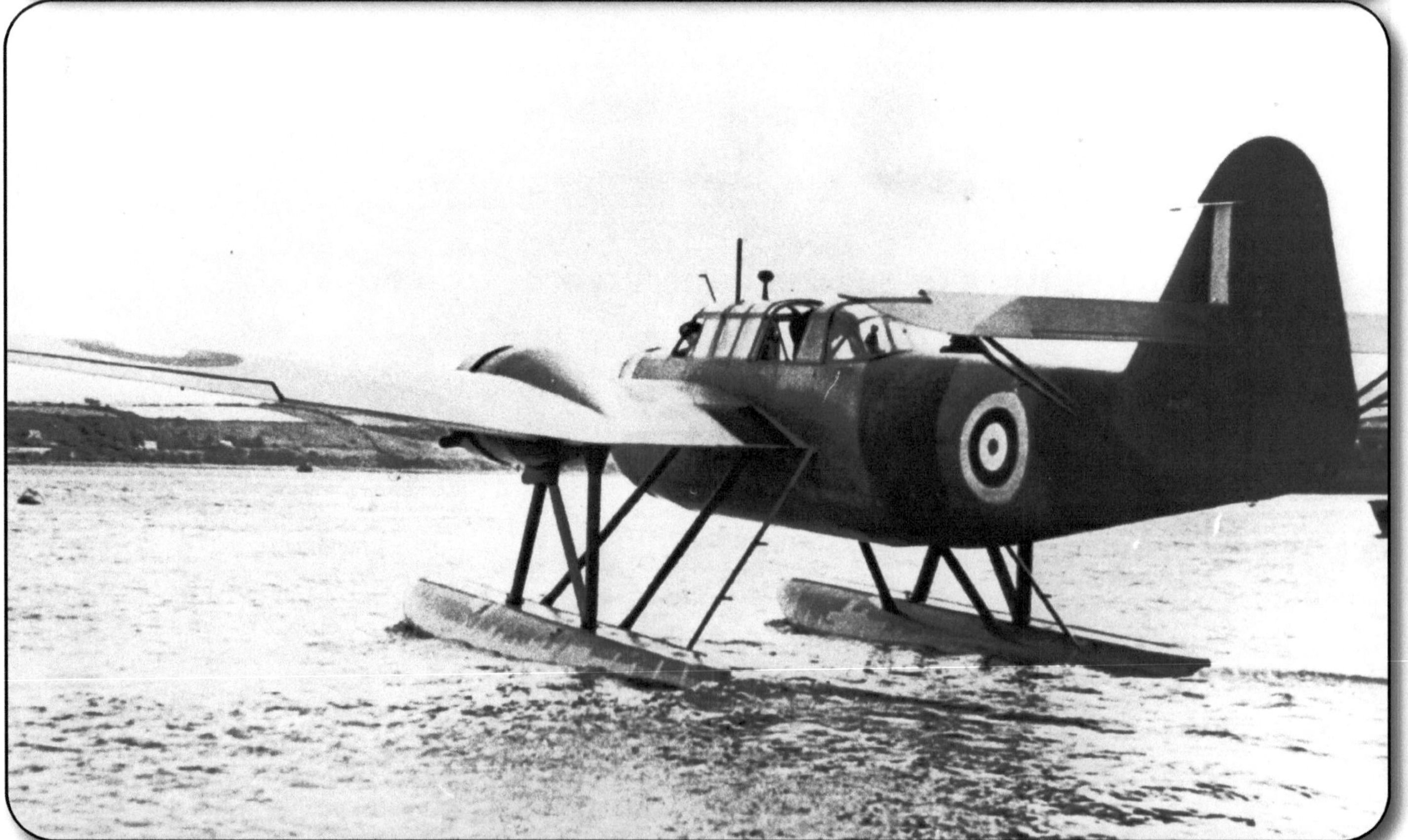

Above, three Fokkers T-VIIIs taken during practice formation flight, Below, one Fokker on the dock ready to be put at sea

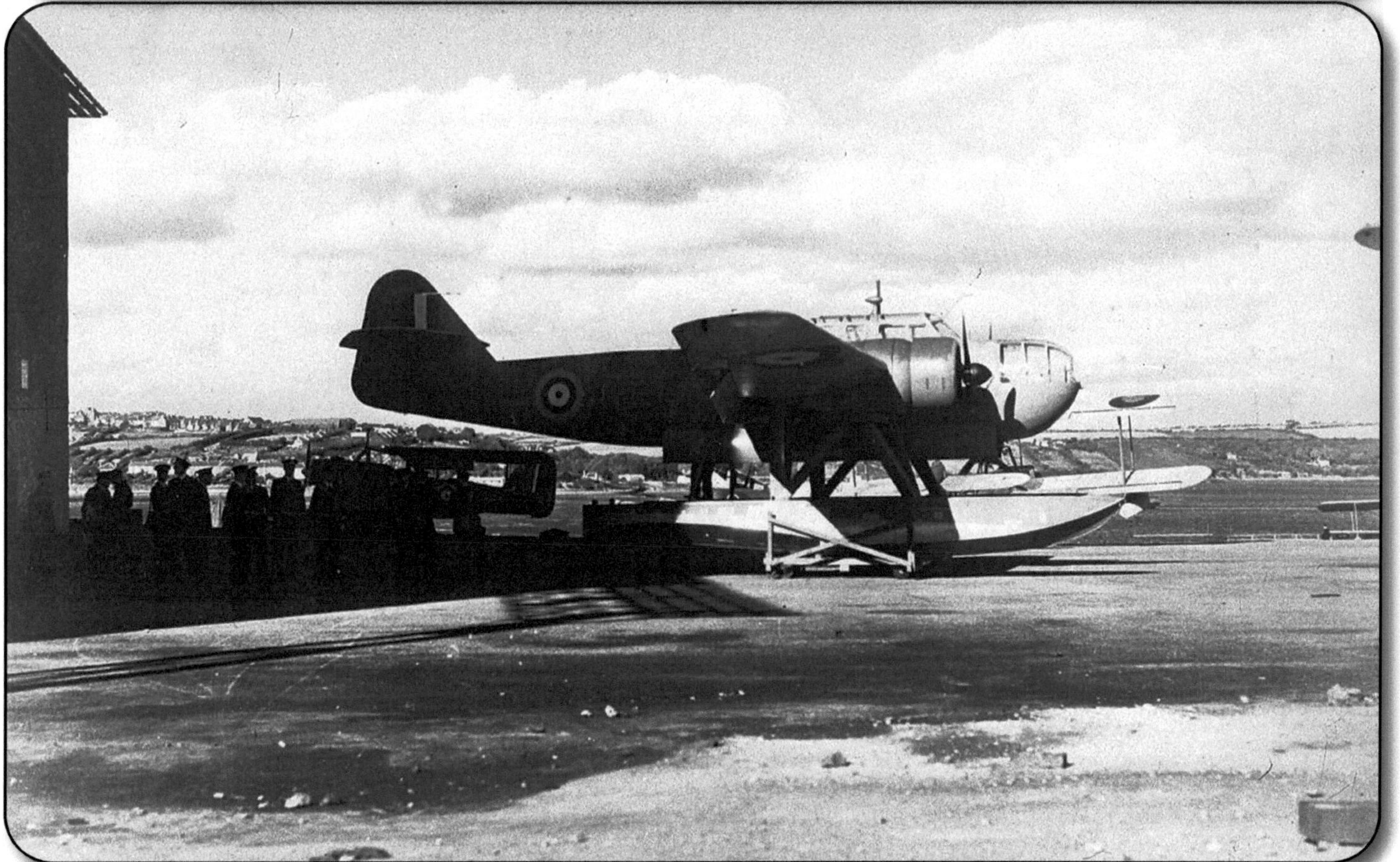

The Northrop N-3PB

With tensions increasing in Europe at the end of the 1930s, and despite the declared neutrality of Norway, the Norwegians followed the global trend to modernise their armed forces, which included the Royal Norwegian Navy Air Service (RNNAS) and the Norwegian Army Air Service. The RNNAS' share was allocated to buy 12 Heinkel 115 torpedo bombers, and 24 reconnaissance aircraft to replace the ageing Marinens Flyvebaatfabrikk M.F.11 biplanes, as well as build several new naval air stations. To replace the M.F.11s, various aircraft, including the Dornier 22, Northrop A-8 and Vultee V-11GB, were considered.

As the Army had already purchased the A-8, a commission was sent to the USA to purchase aircraft and eventually found, in February 1940, a new Northrop project of an A-8 development capable of replacing the M.F.11s. The project was an attack bomber named the N-3 which had improved performance compared to the A-8, increased gross weight and provisions made for ski and water alighting gear. The type caught the commission's attention and negotiations quickly led to an order for an aircraft based on this project, but altered to Norwegian specifications, which called for a floatplane patrol bomber. A contract for 24 aircraft was signed and delivered as the N-3PB (Northrop three-place aircraft, patrol bomber). Despite the fact Northrop had never produced a floatplane, it designed and built the Norwegian prototype in less than eight months. It flew for the first time on 1 November. Meanwhile, however, Germany had invaded Norway on 9 April and had fully occupied the country by the end of June.

Northrop's N-3PB was a three-place, all-metal, low-wing monoplane powered by a single 1,200-hp Wright R-1820 Cyclone engine. Armament consisted of four wing-mounted 0.50-in machine guns, a flexible gun in the rear cockpit and an additional weapon positioned to fire through a trap door under the tail. Northrop took great care to reduce drag as much as possible, including mounting the bulky floats on streamlined single-pillar pylons that had no additional bracing struts or wires. Up to 2,000 pounds of bombs, depth charges or even a torpedo could be carried between the floats. The first N-3PB (301) rolled out of the factory on 13 December 1940 and made its maiden flight on the 22nd from Lake Elsinore, California. The flight-test and customer-acceptance trials were successfully completed using the first production aircraft. Due to the use of the more powerful Cyclone engine, all performance estimates were exceeded and flight characteristics, including handling, were considered excellent. Exiled Norwegians took delivery of their first aircraft on 5 February 1941. Later that month, the first six aircraft were flown from Lake Elsinore to Patricia Bay, near Vancouver, Canada, where training on the type by former naval airmen would take place during the winter. All 24 aircraft, initially coded 1 to 24 (construction numbers 301 to 324), were delivered rapidly to the Royal Norwegian Navy Air Service by the end of March 1941. In the meantime, training in Canada took its toll: 303 crashed on 21 February 1941 near Vancouver, killing the two men on board and, three weeks later, on 18 March, 305 crashed on take-off from Vancouver, killing two of the three occupants. The four remaining N-3PBs were flown to Toronto in the spring of 1941, when the lake was not frozen, where training continued until the spring of 1942. Then the three survivors were shipped to Iceland to reinforce No. 330 Squadron; the fourth aircraft, 307, had crashed in Toronto Bay on 20 June 1941. While taking off, the Northrop collided with the ferry Sam McBride in Port Race, Toronto Harbor, killing both the student pilot, Tron Harsvik, and his instructor, Lt. Finn Kjos.

The first N-3PB/1 (301) on Lake Elsinore before a test flight. It wears pre-war Norwegian markings and a '1' painted on the fuselage. All the N-3PB's flight-testing phase was conducted with this aircraft.

The same aircraft in flight and on its floats on shore. Note that the wing armament has yet to be installed. With four wing-mounted .50-in machine guns, each with 267 rounds, plus a flexible 0.30-in machine gun each in dorsal and ventral positions, with a total of 2,200 rounds, the N-3PB was very well armed for its category. The only comparable floatplane in European skies was the German Ar 196, which had a smaller bomb load.

Hours of patrol flown: *ca.* **3,360**

Number of sorties: *ca.* **850**

First operational sortie:
23.06.41
Last operational sortie:
25.03.43

Total aircraft written-off: 10

Aircraft lost on operations: 4
Aircraft lost in accidents: 6

Squadron code letters:
GS

(up to June 1942)

COMMANDING OFFICERS				
Cdr Hans Bugge (†)	N. 3	RNN	...	25.04.42
Lt-Cdr Johannes Brinch	N. 22	RNN	26.04.42	12.09.42
Lt-Cdr Tortsein Diesen	N. 7488	RNN	12.09.42	...

By March 1941, an agreement had been reached between Norwegian and British authorities for the placing in Iceland of one maritime squadron equipped with the Northrop patrol bombers (for convoy escort and anti-submarine operations). The squadron would be manned by Norwegian personnel but come under the operational control of Coastal Command; already in process was

N-3PB warming its engine on shore while the crew waits at a safe distance.

N-3PB 322/GS-F off the Icelandic coast. Note the '22' painted over the fin flash. The painting of digits over the fin flash was soon discontinued.

the establishing of land and seaplane bases in Iceland following the country's occupation by British forces on 10 May 1940.

By the spring of 1941, the German U-boats' operational area was expanding far out into the Atlantic, well beyond effective air escort range for merchant convoys. Allied and neutral merchant ship losses were already passing unprecedented figures and Coastal Command was hard pressed for aircraft to counter the German submarine threat, since priority for all new long-range bombers was still being given to the build-up of an offensive bomber force to strike back at Germany. Thus, a maritime squadron of single-engine Northrops was a welcome addition to the Command's resources. The Northrops were to replace a squadron of Fairey Battles, stationed in Iceland since the preceding summer, and supplement a squadron of Lockheed Hudsons and another of Sunderland flying boats; Iceland was shortly to become the base of a small but highly specialized and skilful maritime air force. To operate the N-3PB, No. 330 (Norwegian) Squadron was formed on 25 April 1941 and placed under the command of Cdr Hans Bugge of the Royal Norwegian Navy. It was the first Norwegian squadron formed within the RAF. The first personnel had arrived a bit earlier on the 12th with the task of establishing a base for the squadron to make the necessary preparations for receiving the N-3PB. A constant flow of reinforcements arrived in the following weeks. May was dedicated to getting the 18 N-3PBs, which arrived in the Norwegian steamer SS *Fjordheim* with spares, ammunition and bombs, operational. Unloading began on the 22nd and the Norwegians spent days and nights assembling the Northrops; on 2 June, the first of them was flight tested. Soon after, aircrew training started, something that was vital as none of the Norwegian airmen had been through an OTU. This situation obliged the Norwegians to reserve a significant number of the N-3PBs during this first stage of the unit's existence, subsequently restricting its operational capability. However, on 23 June, the squadron was called to provide escort to a convoy passing a short distance south of Iceland. Two N-3PBs did the job, the first, 18, taking off at 22.25 in the hands of Lt C. Stansberg. The convoy was met off the Reykjanes Peninsula and escorted for about two hours before the aircraft was recalled owing to deteriorating weather. Therefore, the relieving flight was cancelled. On becoming operational, the squadron was split in three flights: A Flight, six aircraft based at Reykjavik; B Flight, three aircraft at Akureyri, in the north of the island; and C Flight, three aircraft at Budareyri in a small fjord surrounded by high mountains on the east coast. B Flight would start operations on 26 July and C Flight on 15 September. It was a slow beginning as, in July, only six more patrols were carried out while two aircraft were lost. On 24 July 1941, the squadron's first operational accident occurred when N-3PB 323 overturned on landing and sank in Fossvogur Bay, the crew of two escaping with only slight injuries. Damaged beyond repair, the aircraft was later recovered and cannibalized for spares. Only six days later, 330 suffered its first fatal training flight when 324/GS-G and its crew of three disappeared without trace.

But in the middle of 1941, the U-Boat threat was very high and in August a large concentration of German U-boats was detected in the waters south and south-east of Iceland. Therefore, a maximum effort was asked of Coastal Command's units based on the island. The Norwegians flew close to 50 patrols, representing over 210 hours, in August. Of these, 12 were carried out on the 28th, 29th and 31st, during which four attacks were delivered on U-boats off Iceland's south coast. The first encounter came on 27 August and involved N3-PB 'A' captained by Qm C. Helgesen. After two hours on patrol, the crew sighted a submarine's conning tower a short distance ahead. Diving from 900 to 50 feet, the Northrop's three depth charges failed to release and, by the time the aircraft came in for its second attack, the U-boat had already submerged. Greatly disappointed by the failure of his attack, the pilot proceeded to carry out a square search of the area in the vicinity of the attack and, only 29 minutes after the first sighting, a U-boat's periscope was spotted half a mile ahead. Diving from 750 feet, the aircraft opened fire with its wing-mounted machine guns, the three 350-lb depth charges being released manually slightly ahead of the point where the peri¬scope was last seen. However, the sea was quite rough and no evidence of damage to the U-boat was observed. Remaining in the vicinity for another 50 minutes, the aircraft dropped a sea marker and then returned to base.

The Norwegians put up three N-3PBs early next morning to follow up on the previous day's attack. Having been airborne for an hour and forty minutes in U/330, Qm H. Holdö sighted a British destroyer, four anti-submarine trawlers and a surfaced U-boat at close range. Believing the U-boat was about to deliver an attack on the British vessels, Holdö dived for an immediate attack, releasing two of his three depth charges which exploded about 50 feet to each side of the U-boat's hull, practically lifting it clear of the surface. While climbing out from the attack, Holdö received a signal from the destroyer saying the U-boat had surrendered and was being taken care of. Unbeknown to the N-3PB crew, the U-boat had already surfaced the previous day and surrendered to an Iceland-based Hudson of No. 269 Squadron, and now awaited a naval boarding party. Much to everyone's relief, this otherwise well executed attack was not to cause any damage to the U-boat, which was subsequently towed to Ice¬land and finally entered service with the Royal Navy as HMS *Graph*, but not before it had provided the British with valuable information on German submarine development and construction. Resuming his patrol, Qm Holdö, some 45 minutes later, sighted the conning tower of another U-boat which he attacked with machine-gun fire and the aircraft's remaining depth charge, but no damage was inflicted as far as could be observed. Returning to base, the aircraft was led astray by its defective Kollsman compass and was already halfway to Greenland by the time the crew realised the error. Barely man¬aging to reach a small fishing village on Iceland's west coast before the aircraft ran out of fuel, Holdö had been airborne for seven hours and 20 minutes, compared to the normal estimated seven hours. That was, however, well over the average of about five-and-a-half hours.

During the following months, A Flight continued its convoy escorts and anti-submarine sweeps to the south and south-west of Iceland without engaging the enemy, except on one inconclusive occasion. On 16 September, N-3PB 311/GS-B was damaged beyond economic repair when depth charges accidentally released and exploded while the aircraft was moored at Budareyri while, five weeks later, 315/GS-L crashed on take-off for a training flight on 22 October. There were no casualties. Meanwhile, following Germany's attack on Russia in June 1941, the Allies initiated the Arctic convoy route, and it was soon to become the task of 330 to

N-3PB 310/GS-B seen here being prepared to enter the water.

Top and below: scenes
of the N-3PB in Iceland
during the summer.
Below, two N-3PBs
during the winter at
Budareyri where C Flight
was based. It is easy to
imagine that flying in
such weather conditions
for a single-engine air-
craft could be dramatic if
an engine failure led to
an emergency alighting
in rough seas. The chan-
ce of survival for the
crew was nil.

The N-3PB was not only used for patrol duties but also in various secondary tasks like humanitarian duties. Here, an ill female civilian has been brought in for transfer to the hospital at Reykjavik.

escort the convoys carrying Russia's vital military supplies. Assembling in Iceland, these convoys were escorted by A Flight along Iceland's west coast and through the Den¬mark Strait, where B Flight's aircraft took over, often escorting the convoys hundreds of miles north of the Arctic Circle; the final 500 miles to Murmansk could not be covered by Allied aircraft in 1942 and the convoys were on their own once they left Jan Mayen Island behind. Although primarily employed on convoy escort and anti-sub¬marine duties, the N-3PBs were also called upon to perform a host of other tasks, such as Army co-operation, transport and ambulance flying, air-sea rescue and ice reconnaissance; in fact, any task to which an aircraft could be subjected. At the same time, B Flight at Akureyri spent long hours patrolling the Denmark Strait for enemy surface raiders attempting to break out into the Atlantic while C Flight's aircraft at Budareyri covered the Northern Passage route between Iceland and the Faroe Islands.

Once the Arctic convoys started sailing from Iceland to northern Russia, the frequency of German reconnaissance aircraft operating from bases within occupied Norway to Iceland increased markedly. It was soon to become the task of B and C Flights to put up fighter patrols to counter this latest threat. This was unique in Coastal Command doctrine, the Northrops being the only aircraft of the Command capable of such flights. Indeed, armed with its four 0.50-in fixed guns and two 0.30-in flexible guns, the seaplanes had a formidable concentration of firepower capable of shooting down any German reconnaissance aircraft, even though its lack of speed left little chance of getting close enough to engage successfully. On several occasions, how¬ever, the N-3PBs got in close enough to open fire on the intruders, but none of these engagements were rewarded with any claims.

In 1942, the N-3PBs carried out over 650 sorties and flew 2,500 hours, a significant figure. This, however, was not done without cost. The first N-3PB to be lost was 321/GS-E of C Flight, which crashed on return from patrol on 4 February; one crewman was injured. On 25 April, the CO failed to return from an anti-submarine sweep. No trace of the aircraft was ever found despite an intensive search, he was replaced by the B Flight CO, Lt-Cdr J. Brinch the next day. On 17 September, 302/GS-N of C Flight was caught in fog during a patrol and crashed at Vatnsnes Peninsula while trying to return to base; the crew of three perished. Two months later, on 4 November, 313/GS-L of B Flight crashed north of Iceland during an escort. It was seen to go into a spin and explode on hitting the water. Only the body of the pilot, Qm A. Taarnevsvik, was recovered. Besides the operational losses, some aircraft were also lost during unrelated ops, like 317/GS-M which crashed while landing at Fossvogur Bay on 22 October upon arrival from Budareyri on a ferry flight; fortunately, there were no casualties. Also, 304/GS-V crashed on take-off for a training flight on 24 November; the crew escaped injury, but the aircraft was wrecked. However, because spare parts were a recurrent problem, 308 was withdrawn from use and cannibalised.

The end was near for the N-3PB. Starting from June 1942, A and B Flights began to re-equip with Catalinas, which became operational during the summer. Both flights continued to fly the Northrops on operations alongside the Catalinas until they were disban-

N-3PB 316/S during the summer of 1942. Following the new regulations for Coastal Command squadrons, tactical codes were reduced to a single letter.

ded in December. Only C Flight remained at Budarayri (and the maintenance section). In January 1943, the squadron moved to Scotland, leaving C Flight to continue its patrols. By that time, spare parts had become a major issue and disbandment gave the opportunity to build up stocks by withdrawing several N-3PBs (309, 310 and 312). N-3PB 316 followed in January 1943. C Flight was eventually disbanded at the end of March 1943, having only flown about 15 patrols and 70 hours since the beginning of the year. The last two patrols were flown on 25 March by 318 and 322, the last two operational N-3PBs; since January, all others had been progressively withdrawn from use.

By the spring of 1943, the bulk of the squadron had moved to Scotland where Sunderlands were received. In the meantime, in Iceland in April and May 1943, a number of N-3PBs were transferred from Akureyri and Budareiry to Reykjavik to be stored and eventually scrapped. On 21 April, N-3PB 320/U, took off from Budareiry for Reykjavik. The pilot was Lt Wsewolod Bulukin and the wireless operator was Qm Leif Rustad. En route to Reykjavik, the crew encountered heavy snow showers. They were forced to land on the glacial river Thjorsa. The aircraft was wrecked during the landing. Fortunately, both crew members swam ashore to safety and were able to get back to their squadron within a few days. Meanwhile, back in the river, the N-3PB sank into the mud and water (the wreck was recovered in 1979, restored by Northrop in California and donated to Norway where it remains on museum display). In almost two years of operations, the N3-PB had flown about 850 operational sorties, representing about 3,360 operational hours, all in very tough weather conditions for a large part of the year, not bad for an aircraft which hadn't been developed for such missions as it was intended to only patrol over the Norwegian fjords. The cost was high; of the 24 N-3PBs built, four were lost on operations and six in accidents while serving with 330 while four more were lost in various accident.

N-3PB 309/K on the water at the end of Summer 1942. It was used by B Flight at the time.

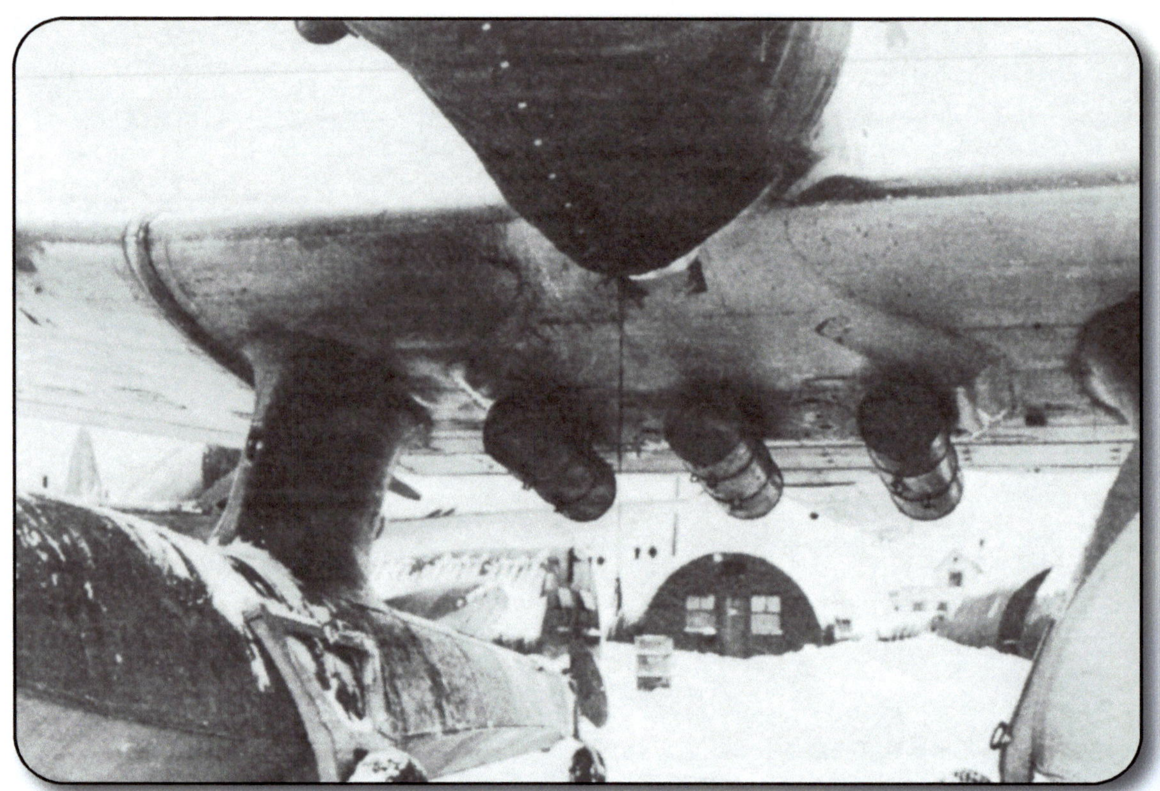

A view of the standard bomb-load arrangement of three 350-lb depth charges mounted on three bomb racks under the centre section of the fuselage. For shipping strikes, the N-3PB could carry 500-lb bombs instead of the 350-lb depth charges.

KNOWN NUMBER OF SORTIES AND OPERATIONAL HOURS COMPLETED BY EACH N-3PB

Serial	code	First sortie	Last sortie	Nbr sorties	Op.hours	Comment
301	A	22.04.42	25.04.42	2	3.6	Lost
302*	N	04.07.42	17.09.42	21	69.7	Lost
303	-	-	-	-	-	
304	V	25.04.42	23.11.42	33	135.3	Lost
305	-	-	-	-	-	
306	K	04.07.42	22.10.42	38	142.1	
307	-	-	-	-	-	
308	A	09.07.41	22.12.41	22	96.2	
309	K	20.08.41	27.05.42	47	193.8	
310	B	10.10.41	11.12.42	73	288.5	
311	B	13.08.41	15.09.41	10	40.6	Lost/acc.
312	D	09.07.41	17.11.42	71	292.0	
313	L	04.01.42	20.10.42	54	231.5	
314*	E	22.02.42	06.02.43	68	262.7	
315	L	26.07.41	02.10.41	6	23.2	Lost/acc.
316	S	18.08.41	29.11.42	64	232.9	
317	M	26.07.41	18.10.42	67	259.4	Lost/acc.
318*	T	23.06.41	24.03.43	73	295.9	
319	G	29.08.41	20.01.43	52	174.2	
320*	U	05.08.41	12.03.43	77	341.8	
321	E	30.07.41	04.02.42	28	106.9	Lost
322	F	27.10.41	25.05.43	44	171.1	
323	-	-	-	-	-	
324	G	-	-	-	-	Lost/acc.
Total				850	3361.4	

*some data are missing regarding the hours flown

Summary of the aircraft lost on Operations - 330 (Norwegian) Squadron

Date	Pilot	S/N	Origin	Serial	Code	Fate
04.02.42	Qm Toralf **HALVORSEN**	N. 7126	RNN	321	GS-E	-
	Qm Einar **GJERTSEN**	N. 35	RNN			-
	Qm **AARSETHER**	N.	RNN			-
25.04.42	Cdr Hans **BUGGE**	N. 3	RNN	301	GS-A	†
	Qm Frithjof **WHIST**	N. 89	RNN			†
	Qm Ståle **PEDERSEN**	N. 158	RNN			†
17.09.42	S/Lt Eilif **VON KROGH**	N. 29	RNN	302	N	†
	Qm Skajalg **LILJEDAL**	N. 458	RNN			†
	Qm Kristian **SIVERTSEN**	N. 5088	RNN			†
04.11.42	Qm Arne **TAARNESVIK**	N. 270	RNN	313	L	†
	S/Lt Einar **GJERTSEN**	N. 35	RNN			†
	Qm Torolf **OSLAND**	N. 5037	RNN			†

Total: 4

Summary of the aircraft lost by accident - 330 (Norwegian) Squadron

Date	Pilot	S/N	Origin	Serial	Code	Fate
24.07.41	Lt Torstein **DIESEN**	N. 7488	RNN	323		-
	Unrecorded					-
30.07.41	S/Lt Carl **VON HANNO**	N. 320	RNN	324	GS-G	†
	Qm Agnar **HANSEN**	N. 125	RNN			†
	Qm Odd **BATALDEN**	N. 18	RNF			†
16.09.41	*Mooring accident*	-	-	311	GS-B	-
22.10.41	Lt Per **HEKTOEN**	N. 8	RNN	315	GS-L	-
	Rest of the crew unrecorded but safe.					
22.10.42	*No details available but crew safe*			317	M	-
24.11.42	Lt Lorentz **SOLBERG**	N.10	RNN	304	V	-
	Rest of the crew unrecorded but safe.					-

Total: 6

THE DORNIER 22

In 1934, the Dornier Company began work on a three-seat multi-purpose military monoplane intended solely for export and suitable for operations on float, wheeled or ski undercarriages. Designated Do 22, the prototype flew for the first time in 1935 as a twin-float seaplane.

A three-seat, high-wing braced monoplane, the Do 22 was powered by an Hispano-Suiza 12Ybrs 12-cylinder liquid-cooled engine rated at 775 hp for take-off and 860 hp at 13,120 feet. The metal, two-spar fabric-covered wing was braced to a tubular structure on the sides of the fuselage, to which could be attached wheels, floats or skis. The fabric-covered, oval-section welded steel-tube fuselage incorporated a tunnel beneath the rear cockpit from which a ventral machine gun could be fired. Single or twin machine guns could be mounted on a Scarff ring over the rear cockpit and a fixed gun could be fitted to fire through the propeller. One torpedo or four 50-kg bombs could be carried. The three cockpits were mounted in tandem, the pilot's cockpit being situated beneath a cutout in the wing's centre section; a folding transparent cover was provided for the centre cockpit which housed the observer, who had access to a second set of controls.

The Do 22 soon attracted orders. The first came from Yugoslavia, for 12 examples of the twin-float version, which was placed on behalf of the Royal Yugoslav Naval Air Service (Do 22Kjs, coded 302 to 313). It was soon followed by a similar order from Greece (Do 22Kg) and another four from the Latvian Government (Do 22Kl); the latter were never delivered and eventually partially found their way to Finland in 1942. The first production Do 22 floatplane was flown on 15 July 1938 and deliveries to Yugoslavia began before the end of the year, followed in 1939 by deliveries to Greece. The first landplane, the Do 22L (D-OXWD), was flown on 10 March 1939, but no orders for this version were received.

The aircraft delivered to Greece equipped the 12th Naval Co-operation Squadron which had ten Do 22s on strength when the country was invaded by Italian forces. Most were lost in action during the weeks that followed, but the fate of the Yugoslavian Do 22s would be different.

In 1941, the 12 Do 22s were split evenly between two units: 20th Hydroplane Squadron at Orahovac and the 25th Hydroplane Squadron at Zlarin i Višovac. The invasion was quick but eight of the 12 Yugoslav machines managed to reach Egypt in April 1941 with their crews (302, 306, 307, 308, 309, 311, 312 and 313).

Upon their arrival, they were allocated RAF serial numbers, **AX708 to AX715**, but it is not clear if they were ever identified as such. Indeed, it seems they flew with the RAF wearing their former serials. To operate the Do 22, No. 2 (Yugoslav) Squadron was formed and placed under No. 230 Squadron's authority at Aboukir, near Alexandria. Because of their short range, the Dorniers could not operate very far from base, so they were used for coastal patrols around the strategic port.

Dornier 22 306 off Alexandria and about to take-off for another anti-submarine patrol armed with depth charges. *(Andrew Thomas)*

After some refresher and practice flights, the Dorniers were ready to start operations at the end of May and the first patrols were carried out on 3 June. From that date, the sorties became more or less daily, but with no more than two aircraft. Usually, the anti-submarine patrols lasted between two and two-and-a-half hours and almost always in the beginning of the afternoon. While the main task of the Do 22s was patrolling off the coast, they were sometimes called to search for missing aircraft. From the start, the Yugoslavians and British knew availability of spare parts would be a major issue. The Dorniers were maintained as best as possible, but availability progressively dropped, a situation made worse with the loss of some aircraft. On 26 August, Do 22 311/AX713 experienced an engine failure during a patrol and ditched 75 metres off Alexandria. The crew, W/O I Korosa and Sgt R Filipovic, was picked up safely by a destroyer later in the evening. On 11 October, the Do 22s were called to search for a missing Blenheim when 312/AX714 suffered an engine failure and made a forced landing off Burg el Arab; it eventually foundered after Lt M. Protic and Lt Ivkovic had been picked up by a destroyer. A few days later, 302 was struck off charge after having served for weeks as a spare parts source, a logical choice as it was a bit different to the others in having a four-blade propeller and a retractable radiator. The squadron continued its operations with five Do 22s but operational activity was, as anticipated, soon reduced to one patrol per day between mid-January 1942 and end of March. In April, the situation improved and two patrols were flown daily. However, the lack of spare parts and the obsolescence of the type led to the disbandment of No. 2 (Yugoslav) Squadron on 23 April. The day before, a final patrol was flown by S/L L Ankon and his crew. Despite its obsolescence and lack of spare parts, and a period of service which lasted less than a year, the Do 22s managed to fly almost 500 sorties for over 1,200 hours of operational flying.

KNOWN NUMBER OF SORTIES COMPLETED BY EACH DO22

Serial	Former	First sortie*	Last sortie	Nbr sorties*	Op.hours	Comment
AX708	302	?	27.11.41	2	4.9	
AX709	306	?	17.02.42	73	189.4	
AX710	307	?	22.04.42	73	174.2	
AX711	308	?	23.02.42	99	255.7	
AX712	309	?	18.04.42	91	231.1	
AX713	311	?	26.08.41	24	50.3	Lost
AX714	312	?	11.10.41	22	52.2	Lost
AX715	313	?	18.04.42	66	159.2	
Not allocated (June 1941)				43	97.7	
Total				493	1214.7	

*No serials are available for June 1941, the first month of operations

Dornier 307 on the shore with a badly damaged wingtip; as it is carrying depth charges, it must have been damaged during an operational sortie. What and when it happened is not known owing to a lack of documentation, but, if 230 Squadron records are to be believed, 307 continued to fly regularly until the disbandment of 2 (Y) Squadron. So, it is logical to assume it was repaired using parts from grounded Do 22s. (Andrew Thomas)

THE VOUGHT OS2U KINGFISHER

By the mid-1930s, the United States Navy (USN) was looking to replace its biplane Curtiss SOC Seagull, a scout-observation seaplane used on board battleships and cruisers. This time, the USN was looking for a more modern aircraft, the trend being to a monoplane configuration.

In 1938, Vought came up with the VS.310, which first flew in 1938 as the XOS2U-1 powered by the reliable 450-hp Pratt & Whitney R-985-4 Wasp Junior. The prototype was provisioned to carry a single 0.30-in machine gun firing between the engine's cylinder heads, and the radio operator manned a 0.30-in on a flexible Scarff ring mount in the rear; underwing pods could carry two 100-lb (45-kg) bombs or 325-lb (147-kg) depth charges. The design was also interesting as Vought devised a simple plug-in system to quickly remove the floats and fit a fixed undercarriage, a configuration little used in service. Satisfied by the various tests, the USN eventually placed an order for 54 production aircraft, as the OS2U-1 Kingfisher, identical to the prototype but with a more refined engine, the -48 version of the Wasp Junior. This version was followed by the -2, of which 158 were built in 1940 with minor alterations. The bulk of production was represented by the -3, which made its debut in 1941. Similar to the -2, the -3 had self-sealing fuel tanks, pilot armour, two 0.30-in guns (dorsal and nose mounted), provision for bombs or depth charges, and the R-985-AN2 engine. In all, 1,006 were built to which 300 OS2N-1s, the Naval Aircraft Factory's variant of the -3, must be added. They equipped nearly all battleships after 1941, and most cruisers of the USN, until 1945. An improved version, the XOS2U-4, was never built.

As it was a specialised aircraft, the Kingfisher was not widely used outside the US. The first nation to do so was the Netherlands, for use in the Netherlands East Indies (NEI), with 24 aircraft purchased. The Royal Navy's Fleet Air Arm received 100 OS2U-3s, as the Kingfisher Mk.I, from March 1942 under the Lend-Lease Act, while Chile, Cuba, Mexico and Uruguay received, via the same channel, a handful of aircraft each; 20 were also supplied to the Soviets.

The first OS2U-1, BuNo 1681, during a test flight in August 1940 before delivery to the USN.

Intense activity at Rathmines during the summer of 1942 which saw the Kingfisher's debut with the RAAF. In the foreground is A48-8, which was lost in January 1943 while serving with the recently formed No. 3 OTU.

KINGFISHER FOR THE RAAF

With the Japanese threat increasing in 1940, the Dutch expressed the need to reinforce their military forces in the NEI. While the Netherlands was initially able to supply most of the demands, when the country fell into German hands, the NEI had no choice but to find another supplier. A large quantity of weapons was bought in 1940 and 1941, including 24 Vought OS2U-3 floatplanes to replace obsolete Dutch types. The new aircraft received the NEI codes V-1 to V-24.

When the Japanese attacked in the Pacific, and the NEI was about to fall, the 24 floatplanes were still en route to the islands aboard three Dutch vessels. They never reached their destination as, once the NEI were overrun, they were diverted to Australia. Needing aircraft of all kinds, the Royal Australian Air Force (RAAF) pressed the Australian Government to make a deal with the Dutch to integrate some Kingfishers into the RAAF's inventory. Following discussions on 9 April, it was decided that six Kingfishers would be allotted to the RAAF's Seaplane Training Flight (SFT) at Rathmines, New South Wales, while another six would be sent to Nouméa in French Caledonia for American use. The balance would be held in storage in Australia. Receiving serials starting with A48, the first six were progressively put into service from 27 April 1942. During the year, all the remaining Kingfishers were eventually erected and joined the SFT's inventory until it was raised as No. 3 OTU on 28 December 1942. Two weeks later, on 14 January, the RAAF experienced its first Kingfisher loss when, after an engine failure, possibly due to lack of fuel, A48-8 was obliged to make a forced landing at sea; it did not go well as the aircraft turned over and sank within 30 seconds. Fortunately, the crew was safe. This was the only loss sustained by the RAAF while using the Kingfisher with a training unit. Indeed, in light of increasing Japanese submarine attacks along the eastern coast of Australia in the last weeks of 1942, the Kingfisher was considered for use as coastal patrol aircraft. Therefore, a squadron, No. 107, was formed on 10 May 1943 at Rathmines with all the remaining Kingfishers still held by the RAAF, 17, to build up a strength of 12 aircraft plus five in reserve. The squadron actually began operations before the official date of formation as all the Kingfishers and most of the personnel were already on hand, the only change was the instructor, normally seated in the back, being replaced by a wireless operator/air gunner. While the Kingfisher had occasionally fulfilled the role of patrol aircraft with 3 OTU during practice flights, it was only when 107 was raised that the seaplanes were officially used as combat aircraft. The squadron's first patrols were flown ten days before its official date of formation, on 1 May; A48-17 and A48-16, flown respectively by F/O V.A. Hiles and P/O V.A. Lucas, flew one patrol each. The Kingfisher could fly for about five hours; most normal patrols lasted between four and five hours. By the end of May, 82 patrols had been flown for around 330 operational hours. However, unknown to the Australians, owing to a combination of bad weather and orders for the Japanese submarines to return north, June saw the end of the attacks which had accounted for 11 sinkings in four months. However, the shortage of aircraft for anti-submarine patrols and convoy escort work led to 107 Squadron remaining in this role for the rest of the war. Nevertheless, it must be said the Kingfisher was not an ideal aircraft for this kind of task because of its lack of speed, giving any submarine the chance to dive before being attacked, and its

Kingfishers dispersed among the trees at Rathmines at the time No. 107 Squadron had been formed. In the forefront, A48-11 which was coded JE-M and behind A48-4 which was coded JE-E.

small bomb load (two 100-lb bombs). Even though improvements rendered the Kingfishers lighter, and therefore faster and capable of carrying 250-lbs bombs, the type remained an inadequate, albeit useful, solution.

After over 1,400 sorties and 5,400 hours of patrols flown from Rathmines, 107 moved to a new base in July 1944, St Georges Basin in New South Wales, to give more room to No. 11 Squadron and its Catalinas. The move was done minus two Kingfishers, which had been lost in the meantime. On 22 September 1943, A48-16 was forced to make a forced alighting at sea; while carrying out gunnery practice off broken bay a round exploded in the breech, the aircraft caught fire and an emergency alighting was performed, damaging the starboard wing tip float; it ultimately capsized. Then, on 4 December, P/O K.J. Dusting was obliged to make a forced landing immediately after take-off for a training flight when the control column jammed. The Kingfisher hit the water right wing down, losing the right float, and rolled over. Happily, in both cases, no injuries were reported by the crews. Patrols resumed on 6 December with three flown. Routine was the key word for 1944. However, the sinking of the US Liberty Ship *Robert J Walker* on Christmas Day 1944 broke this routine. The ship was sunk by a German U-Boat, U-862, south of Jervis Bay, forcing 107 to fly five sorties a day for the next week. On the 26th, F/L OdeV O'Reilly, testing A48-4, believed he sighted the conning tower of a submarine but, because he was not carrying depth charges, an attack could not be made. On 29 December, W/O H.T. Moores carried out the only intentional attack by an Australian Kingfisher of the war; sighting the wake of a periscope in the same area where *Robert J Walker* had been sunk, he attacked with both depth charges. Oil was seen to rise for an hour later, until it covered an area of approximately a quarter mile in diameter, but it was not the U-862 which was attacked; more probably, he had bombed the wreckage of the Liberty ship. The rate of anti-submarine patrols decreased in 1945, logically as the war was now very far from Australian shores. On 23 July, 107 carried out its last two patrols, finishing with an overall respectable tally of close to 2,000 sorties and 7,500 hours of patrols flown. The Australian Kingfishers' little war was over. The squadron ceased operational activity on 1 August and disbandment immediately began, ultimately completed on 28 October. By that time, 13 Kingfishers remained; all were stored. The missing aircraft were A48-1, which had been lost the previous 1 May when it capsized while mooring and was converted to spares, and A48-10, which had been wrecked after alighting on glassy water on 4 October; the Kingfisher hit a swell while still in a flying attitude. The pilot, P/O A.M. Larsen, was seriously injured and the other crewman, P/O D.R. Fisher, was slightly injured.

Various Kingfishers taken during a training flight or a patrol along the New South Wales coastline.
Top: A48-15/JE-Q. Middle, A48-9/JE-K, and a formation of three Kingfishers now stripped of their paint and left in bare metal. Leading is A48-9/JE-K, followed by A48-6/JE-G, A48-14/JE-P and A48-13/JE-O.
(AHM of WA)

Above: A48-5/JE-F and A48-6/JE-G in formation. Below: A48-12/JE-N taking off. *(AHM of WA)*

KNOWN NUMBER OF SORTIES COMPLETED BY EACH KINGFISHER

Serial	Codes	First sortie	Last sortie	Nbr sorties*	Op.hours	Comment
A48-1	JE-A	29.03.44	29.03.45	46	174.3	
A48-2	JE-B	30.10.43	09.07.45	78	300.2	
A48-3	JE-D	07.10.43	19.07.45	114	443.0	
A48-4	JE-E	07.10.43	24.06.45	134	493.0	
A48-5	JE-F	08.10.43	10.07.45	68	274.1	
A48-6	JE-G	10.11.43	19.07.45	64	231.5	
A48-7	JE-H	03.11.43	04.12.43	6	48.5	
A48-8	-	-	-	-	-	
A48-9	JE-K	22.07.43	23.07.45	108	418.9	
A48-10	JE-L	20.05.43	04.10.44	170	658.9	
A48-11	JE-M	11.05.43	23.07.45	218	845.2	
A48-12	JE-N	06.05.43	24.05.45	161	620.8	
A48-13	JE-O	08.05.43	05.07.45	116	454.2	
A48-14	JE-P	04.05.43	06.07.45	134	501.4	
A48-15	JE-Q	03.05.43	06.07.45	126	485.7	
A48-16	JE-R	01.05.43	20.09.43	50	202.1	
A48-17	JE-S	01.05.43	18.02.45	208	812.1	
A48-18	JE-T	03.05.43	24.05.45	151	593.2	
Not allocated in December 44				18	?	
Total				**1970**	**7557.1**	

Summary of the aircraft lost on Operations - 107 Squadron RAAF

Date	Pilot	S/N	Origin	Serial	Code	Fate
04.10.44	P/O Allan M. **LARSEN**	Aus. 432213	RAAF	**A48-10**	JE-L	-
	P/O Allan McL. **FISHER**	Aus. 410594	RAAF			-
			Total: 1			

Summary of the aircraft lost by accident - 107 Squadron RAAF

Date	Pilot	S/N	Origin	Serial	Code	Fate
22.09.43	F/O Allan M. **BRADSHAW**	Aus. 406711	RAAF	**A48-16**	JE-R	-
	F/Sgt Stanley J. **CHEESMAN**	Aus. 43186	RAAF			-
04.12.43	P/O Kenneth J. **DUSTING**	Aus. 427591	RAAF	**A48-7**	JE-H	-
	P:O Richard C. **CREBBIN**	Aus. 423656	RAAF			-
01.05.45	*Capsized while mooring*	-	-	**A48-1**	JE-A	-
			-			
			Total: 3			

The Rogožarski SIM-XIV-H was a Yugoslavian twin-engine coastal reconnaissance floatplane and light bomber with three crew. It was designed and built at the Rogožarski factory in Belgrade. In all, 19 were built in two versions, the SIM-XIV-H and the SIM-XIV-BH with more powerful engines. When Yugoslavia was occupied, one SIM-XIV-H, 157, managed to reach Egypt after a long trip. Being the sole example of its kind, it was, from the start, found to be impossible to maintain. Despite this, the aircraft received an RAF serial, AX716 (following on from the Do 22s), although it didn't fly much. On 28 August 1941, it was used for an air-sea rescue mission, then for two roughly four-hour patrols in January 1942. On 2 February, it took off for another anti-submarine patrol but ran out of fuel and ditched 20 miles north-west of Alexandria. Flight Sergeants S Pishpeck and KJ Pterovich were killed while the observer, F/Sgt B Inkovitch, managed to get out and swim ashore.

Just for the record, even though the He 115 was a floatplane and several served in RAF markings, they were torpedo bombers, not patrol aircraft. All had fled from Norway, which had introduced the type in Autumn 1939 to the Royal Norwegian Navy Air Service (a captured German He 115B-1 was added in the spring of 1940). Four reached the Scottish coast and became BV184 to BV187 in June 1940. They mainly served on clandestine operations in Europe and the Med:
BV184 (ex-56, He 115A-2) was damaged beyond repair by an explosion during take-off from Wing Bay on 31 May 1942, BV185 (ex-58, He 115A-2) destroyed in air raid at Malta on 9 July 1941, BV186 (ex-52, He 115A-2) stored and eventually scrapped in December 1942, BV187 (ex-64, former German He 115B-1), destroyed at Malta by air raid in March 1942.
(Phil Butler)

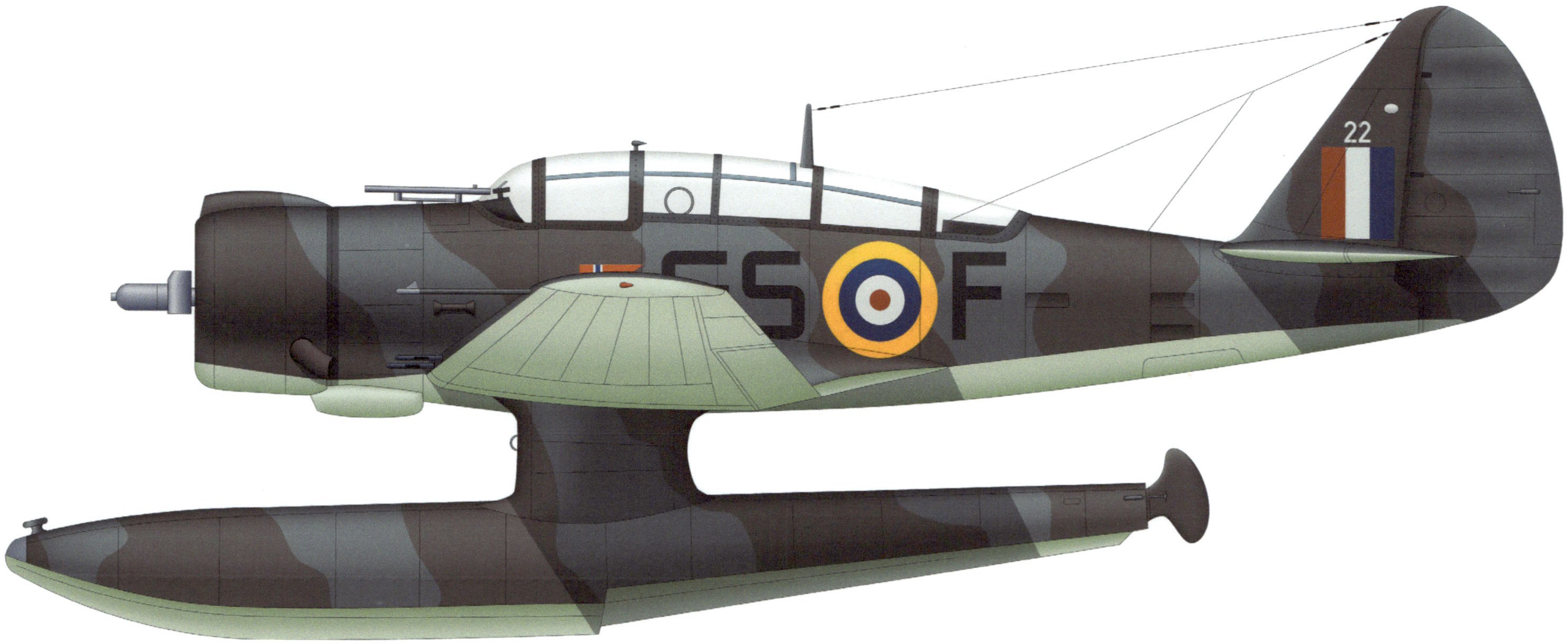

Northrop N-3PB 322
No. 330 (Norwegian) Squadron
Reykjavik (Iceland), summe 1941

Northrop N-3PB 306
No. 330 (Norwegian) Squadron
Akureyti (Iceland), summe 1942

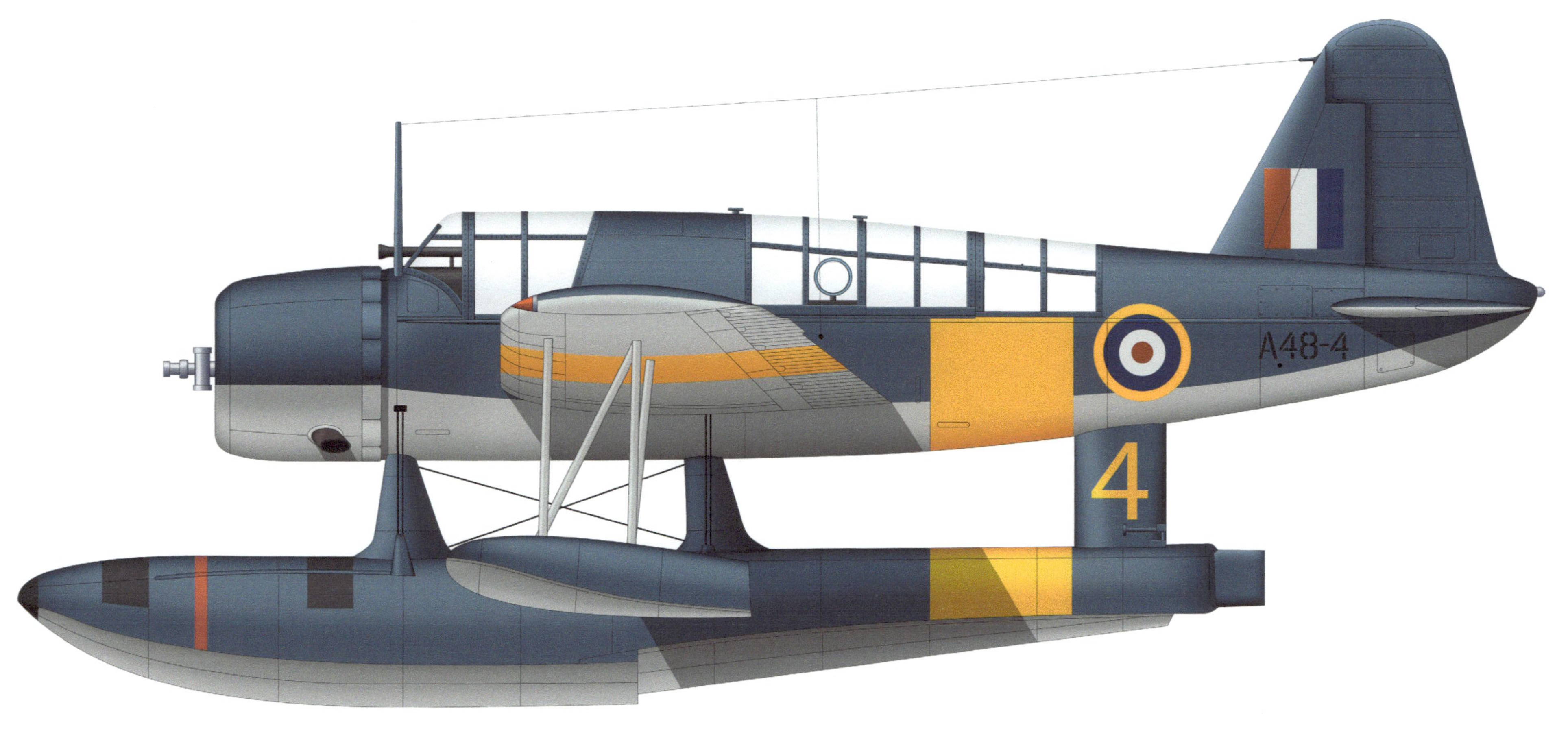

Vought OS2U-3 A48-4
Seaplane Training Flight (STF)
Rathmines (NSW, Australia), autumn 1942

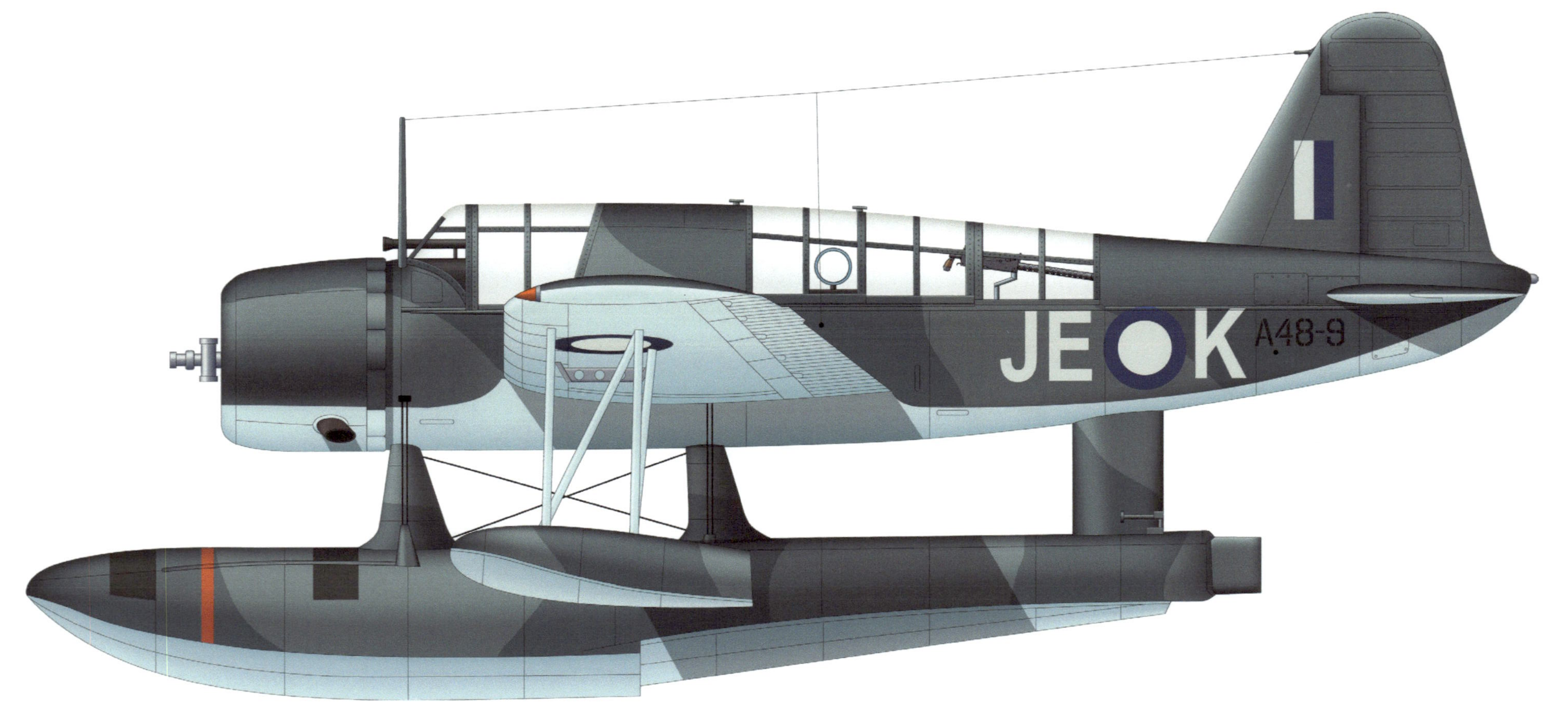

Vought OS2U-3 A48-9
No. 107 Squadron RAAF
St Georges Basin (NSW, Australia), summer 1944

SQUADRONS! - The series